Hot Rods

BY DENNY VON FINN

BELLWETHER MEDIA • MINNEAPOLIS, MN

TORQUE™

Are you ready to take it to the extreme? Torque books thrust you into the action-packed world of sports, vehicles, and adventure. These books may include dirt, smoke, fire, and dangerous stunts.

WARNING: READ AT YOUR OWN RISK.

This edition first published in 2009 by Bellwether Media.

No part of this publication may be reproduced in whole or in part without written permission of the publisher. For information regarding permission, write to Bellwether Media Inc., Attention: Permissions Department, Post Office Box 19349, Minneapolis, MN 55419.

Library of Congress Cataloging-in-Publication Data
Von Finn, Denny.
  Hot rods / by Denny Von Finn.
     p. cm. — (Torque. Cool rides)
  Includes bibliographical references and index.
  Summary: "Amazing photography accompanies engaging information about Hot Rods. The combination of high-interest subject matter and light text is intended for readers in grades 3 through 7"—Provided by publisher.
  ISBN-13: 978-1-60014-210-9 (hardcover : alk. paper)
  ISBN-10: 1-60014-210-9 (hardcover : alk. paper)
  1. Hot rods—Juvenile literature. I. Title.

TL236.3.V66 2009
629.228'6—dc22   2008017017

Contents

What Is a Hot Rod?

Who says something old can't be cool? A hot rod is an old car modified to look low and mean. A **hot rodder** is someone who modifies old cars. Hot rodders change the car's body. They also add a **hopped-up** engine for better speed and acceleration. They paint their hot rod with wild colors and cool designs. Hot rodders create unique cars that show their personality.

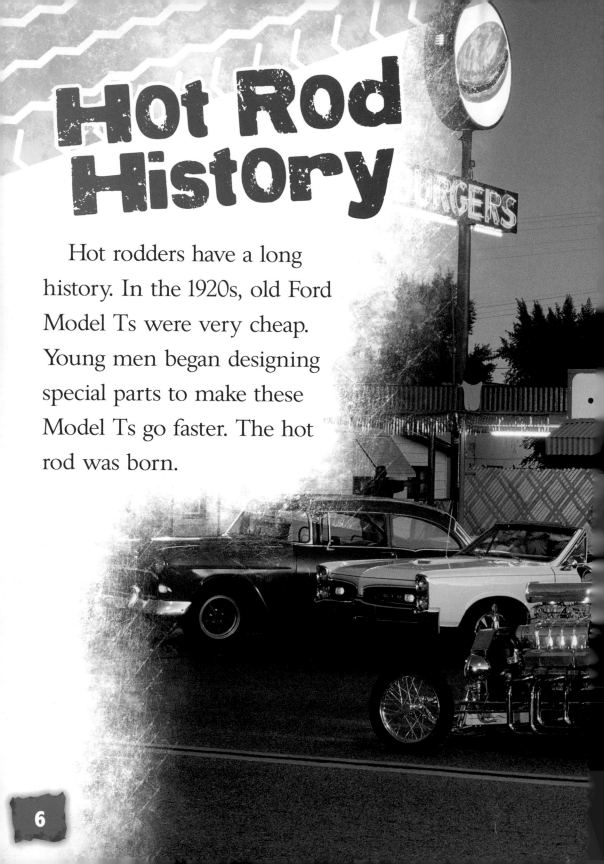

Hot Rod History

Hot rodders have a long history. In the 1920s, old Ford Model Ts were very cheap. Young men began designing special parts to make these Model Ts go faster. The hot rod was born.

In California, many hot rodders raced their **T-buckets** in the flat desert. Unfortunately, some hot rodders also raced on public streets. Street racing was illegal and very dangerous then, just as it is today. In 1951, Wally Parks formed the National Hot Rod Association (NHRA) to promote safety and organize races across the United States.

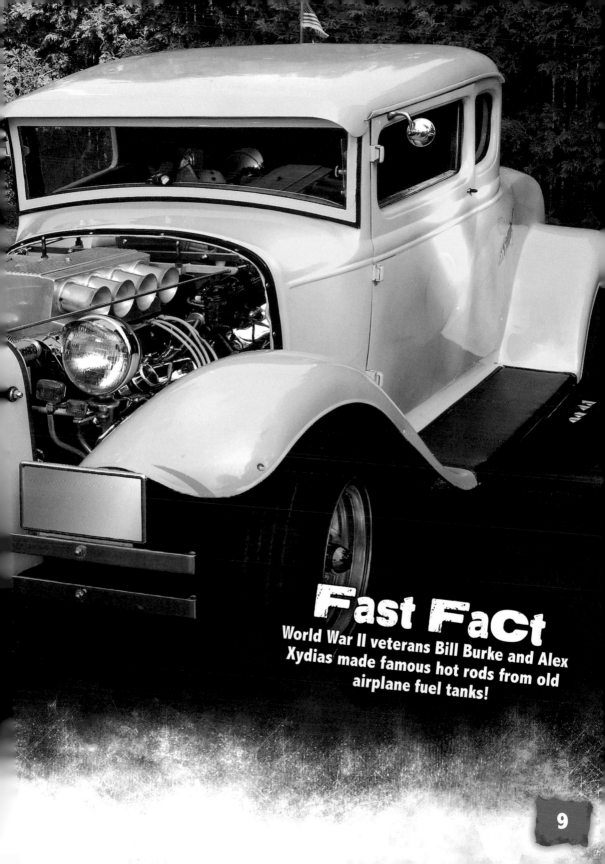

Fast FaCt

World War II veterans Bill Burke and Alex Xydias made famous hot rods from old airplane fuel tanks!

Hot rods became wildly popular in the 1950s. They appeared on TV and in movies. Robert Petersen created successful magazines for hot rodders. Ed "Big Daddy" Roth and others designed hot rods to display at car shows.

Ed "Big Daddy" Roth

Parts Of a Hot Rod

Two kinds of hot rods are the most common. A **roadster** can have a cloth roof that folds down or no roof at all. A **coupe** has a steel roof. Both roadsters and coupes seat just two people.

Fast FaCt

Today, old car bodies are very hard to find. Some companies make fiberglass and steel replicas just for hot rodders.

COLO. 1923

Hot rod bodies are almost always modified. Hot rodders **chop** coupes. The roof supports are cut to lower the roof. Owners often **channel** roadsters. This means the entire body is lowered to sit close to the ground.

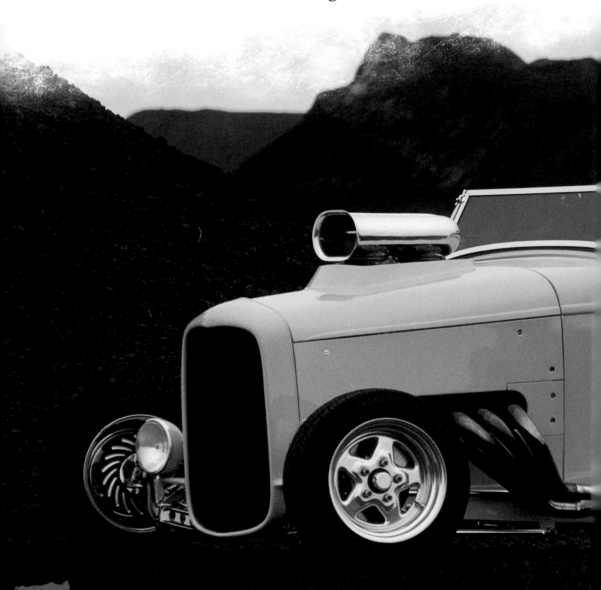

Some owners paint the bodies in bright **metalflake**. Flames and thin painted lines called pinstripes are also popular designs.

Hot rod engines have become more powerful over time. The Ford **Flathead** is the most famous hot rod engine. Car companies such as Chevrolet and Chrysler introduced more powerful engines in the 1950s. Hot rodders began to put Chevrolet and Chrysler engines in their Fords. However, some hot rodders still prefer the older, less-powerful Flatheads today.

Hot Rods in Action

Today's hot rods fall into two categories. Traditional hot rods resemble those from the early days. Their owners prefer vintage parts. Some people call these cars **rat rods** because they are old and rusty. Most traditional hot rodders dislike this term.

A **street rod** is a modern hot rod. Unlike other hot rods, street rods are made from new parts. They also have flashy paint.

Whatever hot rodders enjoy, they can create a hot rod to suit their style.

Glossary

channel—to lower the entire body of a hot rod on its frame so it is lower than normal

chop—to lower the roof of a hot rod

coupe—a two-passenger car with a fixed roof

Flathead—Ford's first eight-cylinder engine, built from 1932 to 1953

hopped-up—describes an engine that is modified to produce more power

hot rodder—someone who builds and drives hot rods

metalflake—a paint with a glittery finish

rat rod—a sometimes negative term used to describe traditional hot rods

roadster—a two-passenger car with a cloth fold-down roof or no roof at all

street rod—a hot rod with modern safety and comfort features

T-bucket—a hot rod made from a Ford Model T

To Learn More

AT THE LIBRARY

Braun, Eric. *Hot Rods*. Minneapolis, Minn.: Lerner, 2007.

Poolos, J. *Wild About Hot Rods*. New York: Powerkids, 2007.

Schuette, Sarah L. *Hot Rods*. Mankato, Minn.: Capstone, 2007.

ON THE WEB

Learning more about hot rods is as easy as 1, 2, 3.

1. Go to www.factsurfer.com

2. Enter "hot rods" into search box.

3. Click the "Surf" button and you will see a list of related web sites.

With factsurfer.com, finding more information is just a click away.

Index

The images in this book are reproduced through the courtesy of: Ian Holland, front cover; Car Culture / Getty Images, pp. 4-5, 6-7, 14-15; Andrew F. Kazmierski, pp. 8-9; Stan Rohrer, p. 10; Time & Life Pictures / Getty Images, p. 11; Oleksiy Maksymenko / Alamy, p. 12; Jdebrod photo, p. 13; Rick Edwards ARPS/ Alamy, pp. 16-17; Don Wilkie, p. 17; Jim Parkin. P. 18; Mark Scheuern / Alamy, p. 19; Chris Curtis, pp. 20-21.